Bad Dad Jokes

A Da-da-Base of Puns, Word Plays, and other Groaners

They sing ... because they can

By Steven P. Hendrix

"Bad Dad Jokes, A Da-Da Base of Puns, Word Plays and other Groaners," compiled by Steven P. Hendrix. ISBN 978-1-63868-075-8 (softcover).

Published 2022 by Virtualbookworm.com Publishing, P.O.Box 9949, College Station, TX, 77842, US.

©2022 Steven P. Hendrix. All rights reserved. No part of this publication may be reproduced, stored in a retrieval system, or transmitted in any form or by any means, electronic, mechanical, recording or otherwise, without the prior written permission of Steven P. Hendrix.

Foreword

I have long collected puns and other jokes, the better to embarrass my children in front of their friends. Bad dad puns -- that's how eye roll. You could say that I wrote the book on bad dad jokes - because you're reading it. It's poor form to tell dad jokes if you're not really a dad, because that would be a faux pa.

I can lay legitimate claim to the title of "Dad". My wife Kathy and I have three children by birth, two by adoption, and we cared for 36 babies over the course of 20 years as foster parents. At one point we had two children in college, one in high school, one in kindergarten, one in preschool, and one in diapers. I thank Kathy and all those kiddos for the richness they've brought into my life.

Acknowledgements

I would like to thank my wife Kathy for making me a dad three times and for supporting me in all my endeavors. I would also like to thank my grandparents for making a dad for me in 1931. And, of course, my parents for raising me with a proper appreciation for puns and other humor, as well as all my kids for the obligatory groan responses, and friends with a proper appreciation for puns, who so often respond to my puns with puns of their own.

Table of Contents

Foreword 1
Acknowledgements 2
Table of Contents 3
Sports 5
Mathematics 8
The Jungle 11
Employment 13
Science 16
Military 18
Food 20
Relationships 23
Holidays 25
Computers 28

Nature	30
Astronomy	33
Entertainment	35
πDay	38
Word Plays	40
Family Life	42
Health	47
Pets	52
Geography	56
School	59
Beekeeping	62
Church	63
Transportation	66
Politics	68
Aviation	70

Sports

I heard a joke about boxing, but I missed the punch line.

I'm trying to organize a hide-and-seek contest, but good players are hard to find.

A limbo champion walked into a bar, and was immediately disqualified.

Cinderella was kicked off the soccer team because she ran away from the ball.

The football coach went to the bank to get his quarter-back.

The lifeguard wouldn't swim out to save the hippie, because he was, like, too far out, man.

My friend Tyler came in first in the Bejing marathon, but still has not been awarded a gold medal. China refuses to acknowledge Ty won.

What runs around a soccer field but never moves? A fence.

How do you make an ice skating rink free of germs? You steril- ice it.

The best way to see a fly fishing contest is to watch the live stream.

They're having a new kind of he-man fishing contest on Lake Erie this year, where you have to catch the fish with your bare hands. They're calling it The Grab-Bass Tournament.

When they flew the horses over to Tokyo for the equestrian events in the Olympics, they called the plane Air Horse One. And if they only put the back end on, it was Air Force One. Then they only go half-fassed. You might get a kick out of that.

Tennis is such a noisy game because each player raises a racket. Because of inflation, we now have to play elevennis.

Who was the fastest runner in history? Adam, first in the human race.

I wondered why the baseball was getting bigger. Then it hit me. The last thing I want to do is hurt you, but it's still on my list.

The chess champions were bragging about their accomplishments in the motel lobby before the tournament. The manager threw them out, saying "I can't stand chess nuts boasting in an open foyer."

Old quarterbacks never die, they just fade back and pass away.

NFL players are not allowed to have a chicken as a pet. That would be a personal fowl.

A chess match between a mind reader and someone who can see the future would glitch the matrix.

You have to be odd to be number one.

Having a dog named Shark at the beach is a bad idea.

Mathematics

Science jokes make me numb. Math jokes make me number.

If Americans switched from pounds to kilograms overnight, there would be mass confusion.

If you're bad at haggling, you'll end up paying the price.

My fingers are very reliable. I can always count on them.

My calendar's days are numbered.

A chicken who counts her eggs is a mathemachicken.

6 was afraid of 7 because 7 8 9. Why did 7 eat 9? He needed 3^2 meals a day.

99.9% of people are idiots. Fortunately, I belong to the 1% of intelligent people.

There are 10 kinds of people – those who understand binary numbers and those who don't.

There's a fine line between numerator and denominator. Only a fraction of people will get the joke.

After the Flood, Noah told all the animals to "go forth, be fruitful, and multiply". All left except a pair of snakes. Noah gave up, and built a picnic table from logs so he and his wife could have a nice quiet meal. As soon as he finished, the snakes took off across the table. They said, "We're adders, we can use a log table to multiply."

"There are two types of people in the world. 1) Those who can extrapolate from incomplete data.

A yard stick is a garden ruler.

Cowculus. 😆

The Jungle

A cannibal is someone who is fed up with people.

We're headed into headhunter territory, which is a terrible place to be headed.

Bigfoot is often confused with Sasquatch, Yeti never complains.

They say a boa constrictor can eat up to 500 pounds at one sitting. I find that very hard to swallow.

The koala bear isn't considered a real bear because it didn't koala-fy.

The king of the jungle told me he was a tiger, but he was lion.

The urge to sing "The Lion Sleeps Tonight" is always just a whim away....a whim away, a whim away, a whim away....

People are crazy about the exterior of that ship named after the bear from Jungle Book. Personally, I'm tired of the hullabaloo.

Animal puns? Toucan play that game.

A lion was fortunate to bring down a male ox all by himself. After thoroughly gorging on the meat he got a tummy-ache and started roaring in pain, nonstop. A hunter heard this and came to shoot him, proving that if you're full of bull you should keep your mouth shut.

Why don't hedgehogs just learn to share the hedge?

I have a fear of giants. It's called feefiphobia.

Employment

I used to work at an orange juice factory, but I got canned. Couldn't concentrate, so they put the squeeze on me.

Elevator jokes are great because they work on so many levels.

Garbage collectors don't need training. They just pick it up as they go.

I used to be a banker but then I lost interest.

I answered the phone and all I heard was sneezing. I hate cold callers.

When I told the contractor I didn't want carpeted steps, he gave me a blank stair.

I got a job making pizza crusts because I kneaded the dough.

My Tinder bio says I have a corner office with views of the entire city, drive a half-million-dollar vehicle, and I'm paid to travel. My dates are never happy when I tell them I'm a bus driver.

I got fired from my job for asking customers whether they prefer "smoking" or "non-smoking". Apparently, the correct terms are "cremation" and "burial".

My friend gets upset when I call him a flat-earther. He says the correct term is bulldozer operator.

What do you do? I race cars. Do you win many races? No, the cars are much faster than me.

If you rearrange the letters of MAILMEN, you get them very angry.

Bart walks into a bar and immediately gets shot and dies. Who killed him? The Bart-ender.

I know a lot of jokes about retired people, but none of them work.

What is the biggest room in the world? Room for improvement.

Despite the high cost of living, it remains popular.

Electricians have to strip to make ends meet.

Some people are wise, some are otherwise.

Police toilet stolen! Cops have nothing to go on!

Forklift operators find our puns unpalletable.

A lot of money is tainted – 'taint yours and 'taint mine.

Who drives away all his customers? A taxi driver!

Buses stop in bus stations. Trains stop in train stations. My desk is a work station.

I know a bailiff who moonlights as a bartender. He serves subpoena coladas.

I heard about a carpenter who varnished without a trace.

A blind man walked into the bank with his white cane held up over his head and said, "This is a stick up."

Old bankers never die, they just lose interest.

The invention of the shovel was groundbreaking, the invention of the broom was the one that truly swept the nation, but the invention of the wheel really got things rolling.

Monkeys just pretend to be less intelligent than humans to avoid paying taxes and going on a job search.

I'm terrified of elevators and I'm taking steps to avoid them.

I pulled a muscle digging for gold. It's just a miner injury.

Ghosts like to ride in elevators because it lifts their spirits.

Science

When chemists die, they barium.

Never trust atoms. They make up everything.

Two hydrogen atoms meet. One says, "I've lost my electron." "Are you sure?" "Yes, I'm positive."

For chemists, alcohol is not a problem, it's a solution.

A burglar stole all the lamps from the school laboratory. We should be upset, but we're delighted.

My least favorite color is purple, I hate it more than red and blue combined.

How does a color laugh? Hue, hue, hue.

Why did the dinosaur stand beside the road? It was waiting to evolve into a chicken.

A neutron walks into the bar and asks, "How much is a beer?" The bartender replies "For you, no charge."

Think like a proton and stay positive.

Resistance is not futile – it's voltage divided by current.

The half-full glass is actually full – 50% water, 50% air.

You matter, unless you multiply yourself by the speed of light squared, and then you energy.

The universe is made of protons, neutrons, electrons, and morons.

Duct tape can't fix stupid, but it can muffle the sound.

Oxygen and magnesium are dating. OMG!

Water is heavier than butane because butane is a lighter fluid.

Broken barometer for sale – no pressure.

Military

A commander walks into a bar and orders everyone around.

An old soldier who survived mustard gas and pepper spray is a seasoned veteran.

War does not determine who is right, only who is left.

I really dislike Velcro. Total rip-off.

How does an octopus go to war? Well armed.

A regiment of military rabbits who have been trained to fly is the Hare Force.

A submarine got caught between two destroyers and they called it a sub sandwich.

Military parachutes come with a money-back guarantee.

An armored vehicle with artificial intelligence is a think tank.

The army can't comprehend the 6-foot social distancing rule, but the navy can certainly fathom it.

A manufacturer makes prayer mats for Muslims. Since 911 they've been including an explosive charge in each one. They say business is booming. Prophets are going thru the roof.

I know a great joke based on the army reserve, but it only works one weekend a month.

A baker in the army goes in with all buns glazing.

Food

Soy milk? No whey!

I ordered a chicken and an egg from Amazon. I'll let you know.

I ate a kid's meal at McDonald's today. His mom got really angry.

I invested in a cannabis-fed cattle business. The steaks have never been higher.

I switched around all the labels on my wife's kitchen spices. I'm not in trouble yet, but the thyme is cumin.

I used to be addicted to soap but I'm clean now.

What kind of tea is the hardest? Reali-tea.

The review of the restaurant on the moon said "Great food, no atmosphere."

What do you call a sad cup of coffee? De−presso.

What do you call a cow with no legs? Ground beef.

I want to tell you a joke about a girl who eats only plants. You've probably never heard of herbivore.

I know a guy who is addicted to brake fluid. He says he can stop any time.

If you boil a funny bone, it becomes a laughing stock. That's humerus, no bones about it.

Ban pre-shredded cheese. Make America grate again.

We're in search of fresh vegetable puns. Lettuce know.

Crushing pop cans is soda pressing.

Dijon vu – the same mustard as before.

Practice safe eating – always use condiments.

A hangover is the wrath of grapes.

A boiled egg in the morning is hard to beat.

Bakers trade bread recipes on a knead-to-know basis.

With two ducks and a cow, you'd have quackers and milk.

Everyone should go to sleep after drinking a cup of tea. When the T is gone, NIGHT becomes NIGH.

Venison for dinner again? Oh deer!

French pancakes give me the crepes.

Jokes about German sausage are the wurst.

When a clock is hungry, it goes back four seconds.

Knowledge is knowing a tomato is a fruit. Wisdom is knowing it doesn't belong in a fruit salad.

I shot a turkey and everyone else in the frozen foods department went crazy.

In rural Ohio people only lock their car doors in July and August, to prevent coming back and finding the back seat full of tomatoes and zucchini.

A cheese factory exploded in France. Da brie is everywhere.

What did the grape say when it got crushed? It just let out a little wine.

A man got hit in the head with a can of Coke, but he was okay because it was a soft drink.

I ate four cans of alphabet soup and just had the largest vowel movement ever.

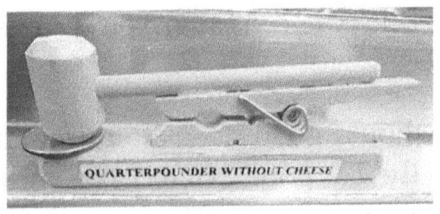

Relationships

I was dating a girl who was cross-eyed, but we had to break it off because we couldn't see eye-to-eye. Besides, I think she was seeing someone on the side.

I was invited by a female janitor to smoke some weed at her apartment, but I can't deal with high maintenance women.

I loaned my girlfriend $100 soon after we met. Three years later we broke up, and she returned exactly $100. I lost interest in that relationship.

I found out my friend is really a ghost. I had my suspicions the moment he walked thru my door.

I'm taking care of my procrastination issues, just you wait and see.

She only made whiskey, but I loved her still.

Shotgun wedding – a case of wife or death.

A man needs a mistress just to break the monogamy.

Dancing cheek-to-cheek is really a form of floor play.

She was engaged to a boyfriend with a wooden leg, but broke it off.

With her marriage she got a new name and a dress.

My girlfriend told me to stop impersonating a flamingo. I had to put my foot down.

Love is blind – but marriage is a real eye-opener.

A hole has been found in the nudist camp wall. Police are looking into it.

I was at a really emotional wedding. Even the cake was in tiers.

Holidays

Presidents' Day is a day to remind us to honor and respect our leaders. Just look at Mt. Rushmore to see what happens when we take them for granite.

From the Geology professor: Oh shist! That's some rock-solid thinking.

Don't laugh at puns about rocks – that will only make him boulder.

Don't rock the boat, it will just cause stonewalling.

If you saw Mt. Rushmore before it was carved, that's truly unpresidented.

Did you **hear the song** about trying to shorten the alphabet? No 'L', no 'L'.

St. Patrick's: What's Irish and stays outside all year? Patty O'furniture.

Never iron a four-leafed clover, because you don't want to press your luck.

I hate that SEPTember, OCTober, NOVember, and DECember aren't the 7th, 8th, 9th, and 10th months. Whoever messed this up should be stabbed.

It's all fun and games till Santa checks the naughty list.

Resolutions. In one year and out the other.

May the fourth is Star Wars Day. The following day commemorates the day the ship full of Hellman's went down.

Santa's helpers are subordinate clauses.

Columbus was the world's first fuel economy nut. He got 4000 miles to the galleon.

When is a rock not a rock? On St. Patrick's Day, when it's a sham-rock.

Santa Claus had the right idea: Visit people only once a year.

How do you catch a unique Easter bunny? You 'neak up on him. How do you catch a tame one? Tame way!

Computers

I named my iPad Titanic, and now it says Titanic is syncing.

Software guys are usually off by one, but analog circuit guys are off by 2π, and digital guys are off by a bit.

Steve Jobs would have made a better president than Trump, but that's comparing apples to oranges.

Why did King Arthur sign up for so many Zoom meetings? He liked to be on cam a lot.

A whiteboard is the most re-markable invention of the last 100 years.

Why is a computer so smart? Because it listens to its motherboard.

I got an email about reading maps backwards. Turned out it was just spam.

You can't use beefstew as a password. It's not stroganoff.

When IBM PC clones came out with double-speed processors, some games didn't work, so the manufacturers added a switch to return to normal PC speed. Soon they found that nobody wanted a half-fast computer.

Eyes hurt from too much screen time? There's a nap for that.

When my battery died, I was angry and needed to find an outlet.

Nature

Is this a dogwood tree? Yes, you can tell by the bark.

What do you call a fly with no wings? A walk.

What do you call a doe with no eyes? No-eye-deer.

What do you call a bear with no teeth? A gummy bear.

What do an 'A' and a flower have in common? They both have B's coming after them.

You can tell an alligator from a crocodile by whether it sees you later or in a while.

I don't usually trust trees; they always seem a bit shady.

When a snowman throws a tantrum, it's a meltdown.

Reading while sunbathing makes you well red.

A dinosaur with an extensive vocabulary is a Thesaurus.

After the fruit was picked, the bruin wandered into the orchard, looking for the bear trees he'd heard were there.

Two fish swim into a concrete wall. One turns to the other and says "dam".

Dust is mud with the juice squeezed out.

A toothache is a pain that drives you to extraction.

My friend Jack learned he could make his garden grow better by talking to his plants. He got so involved in it that they wrote a story, called Jack and the Beans Talk. Such a pun – I'm green with envy.

Dead fish always go with the flow.

The four seasons are all different. Summer warmer than others.

Our scout troop formed a handbell choir to augment the music around the campfire, but when they got to camp, all they could make was tree rings.

The cows returned to the marijuana field, because the pot called the cattle back.

A pod of musical whales is an orca-stra.

What do you call a fish with eight eyes? A fiiiiiiiish.

Dear northern friends: Come get your weather, it's in my driveway.

Before the crowbar was invented, crows had to drink at home.

Astronomy

I'm reading a book about anti-gravity. I can't put it down.

How does the moon cut his hair? 'E clipse it.

I stayed up all night wondering where the sun went, and then it dawned on me.

I am Buzz Aldrin, second man to step on the moon. Neil before me.

6:30 is the best time of day, hands down.

I was going to tell a time travel joke, but you already didn't like it.

The beginning of daylight savings time is a busy night at Stonehenge as the workers move all the stones ahead one hour.

Astronomers got tired of watching the sun go round the earth for 24 hours, so they decided to call it a day.

The moon goes to the bank to change quarters.

What holds the moon in place? Its beams.

Which is heavier, a half-moon or a full-moon? The half-moon, because the full-moon is lighter.

Entertainment

The Black Eyed Peas can sing us a tune, but the chick peas can only hummus one.

Why did the Star Wars movies come out in the sequence 4,5,6,1,2,3? In charge of the sequence, Yoda was.

How do you organize an outer space party? You planet.

Did you hear about the fire at the circus? It was in tents.

The sesame seed wouldn't leave the casino because he was on a roll.

He who laughs last didn't get it.

If you suck at playing the trumpet, that's probably why.

Life without music would B flat.

A midget fortune teller who escapes from prison is a small medium at large.

I like to hold hands in the movie theater, which really startles strangers.

They begin the evening news with "Good Evening", then proceed to tell you why it isn't.

An E-flat, a G-flat, and a B flat walk into a bar. The bartender says, "I don't serve minors".

I was addicted to the hokey-pokey, but I turned myself around.

The inventor of the hokey-pokey died last week. They had trouble keeping his body in the coffin. They'd put his left foot in, he put his left foot out...

Did you hear the song about the tortilla? Actually it was more of a rap.

What kind of music is scary for balloons? Pop music, in a sharp key.

How many first violinists does it take to screw in a light bulb? Just one to hold it in place while the world revolves around them.

How many second violinists does it take to screw in a light bulb? Doesn't matter, they can't get up that high.

What do you call a cow playing an instrument? A moo-sician.

If you dress like a cowboy, are you ranch dressing?

Why did Ariel wear seashells? Because she outgrew B shells.

π Day

When you divide your jack-o-lantern's circumference by its diameter, you get pumpkin π.

When you divide your heifer's girth by her width you get cow π.

Be careful not to mix your pumpkin π with your cow π because that would be irrational.

Who was the fattest knight at King Arthur's round table, and how did he get that way? Sir Kumference; he ate too much π.

A farmer put 96 cows out to pasture. When he rounded them up he had 100. (96 cows plus a cow π "rounds up" to 100,).

Cow π! That stinks!

Once π starts to talk it goes on forever.

When you divide the sun's circumference by its diameter, you get π in the sky. True, it's irrational, but I'll still give you some heat about it.

When March starts on a Sunday, it includes three consecutive days of irrational terror: Friday the 13th, full of superstitions about bad luck, the Ides of March on the 15th, and sandwiched between them, π day 3.14 to terrify math phobes.

I've memorized all the digits of π (0123456789). Still working on the order.

You can't argue with π – it's irrational.

In Jamaica a slice of pie costs $3.50. In the Bahamas, $5.50. These are the π-rates of the Carribean.

My pet snake is 3.14 meters long. He's a π thon.

Apple π was Newton's favorite dessert.

What is the volume of a cheese pie with a thickness of a and a radius of z? Pi * z * z * a!

A secret agent who is good at math and can solve complex equations is a s- π.

When you take a green cheese and divide its circumference by its diameter you get a moon π.

There was a murder in the Math department. They brought in a special investigator named Magnum π.

When this number writes an irrational story of its life, it is an auto-π-ography.

These π jokes go on forever.

Word Plays

The word "nothing" is a palindrome. Backwards it spells "gnihton", which also means nothing.

If "womb" is pronounced "woom," and "tomb" is pronounced "toom," then "bomb" should be pronounced "boom." The English language blows my mind.

I was arrested for downloading Wikipedia in its entirety. Before they took me away, I said "Wait, I can explain everything."

Someone broke in and stole the first 20% of my couch. Ouch!

Are "well" and "actually' single-syllable words? Well, yes, but actually, no.

Spider-Man is so good at comebacks, because with great power comes great response ability.

Have you ever tried to eat a clock? It's really time consuming.

I have a great joke about cliffhangers..........

They said I couldn't be good at poetry because I'm dyslexic. So far I've made 3 jugs and a vase and they are lovely.

I was kidnapped by mimes, and they did unspeakable things to me.

Prison is just one word to you, but for some people, it's a sentence.

Irony is the opposite of wrinkly.

When two egotists meet it's an I for an I.

Time flies like an arrow. Fruit flies like a banana.

A dyslexic man walks into a bra....

I sent ten different puns to my friends, hoping at least one would make them laugh. No pun in ten did.

I before E, except after C. Weird.

Family Life

My wife just completed a 40-week body building program. It's a girl and weighs 7 lbs 8 oz.

Today is the last time I will see my 80-year-old Grandpa. Tomorrow, he turns 81.

If the house is cold go stand in a corner. It's 90° there. That's acute joke.

My daughter said, "What rhymes with orange?" I replied, "No it doesn't."

Where do you take someone who has a peek-a-boo accident? To the ICU.

When I moved into my new igloo, my friends threw me a surprise house-warming party. Now I'm homeless.

How does an Eskimo repair his broken home? Using Ig-glue.

My landlord texted saying we need to meet and talk about how high my heating bill is, so I replied "Sure, my door is always open."

Lance is an uncommon name nowadays, but in medieval times people were named Lance a lot.

As I handed my dad his 50th birthday card, he said "You know, one would have been enough."

My son Luke loves that we named our children after Star Wars characters. My daughter Chewbacca, not so much.

I was shocked when my wife told me our 5-year-old son wasn't actually mine. She said I need to pay more attention at school pick-up.

I was so bored sitting at home that I memorized six pages of the dictionary. I learned Next to Nothing.

I sold my vacuum cleaner. All it was doing was collecting dust.

When you clean your vacuum cleaner, you become a vacuum cleaner.

The other day my wife asked me to pass her lipstick, but I accidentally gave her a glue stick. She still isn't talking to me.

Babies who refuse to sleep during nap time are guilty of resisting a rest.

Balloons are so expensive these days. I blame inflation.

Dad, are we pyromaniacs? Yes, we arson.

I went to the toy store and asked where the Schwarzenegger dolls are. He said, "Aisle B, back."

My wife is still hot. It just comes in flashes now.

If your fridge is running, I'd vote for it.

A man's home is his castle, in a manor of speaking.

You feel stuck with your debt if you can't budge it.

Once you've seen one shopping center, you've seen a mall.

Of course, I run things at my house...the vacuum cleaner, the garbage disposal, etc.

The best thing about the good old days is, we weren't good and we weren't old.

I was raised as an only child, which really annoyed my sister.

There are two theories to arguing with a woman. Neither works.

PMS jokes aren't funny – period.

A married man should forget his mistakes. No use in two people remembering the same thing.

Kids in the back seat cause accidents. Accidents in the back seat cause kids.

The only time the world beats a path to your door is when you're in the bathroom.

It's not hard to meet expenses...they're everywhere.

Where there's a will, I want to be in it.

We never really grow up, we just learn how to act in public.

I didn't say it was your fault. I said I was blaming you.

A clear conscience is the sign of a fuzzy memory.

Nostalgia isn't what it used to be.

Where there's a will, there are relatives.

Our lives are ova before they've begun.

Juan and Amal are identical twins. Their mom only carries one photo, because if you've seen Juan you've seen Amal.

How long does it take for a boy scout to change a light bulb? About a week, if he gives it one good turn daily.

Their son was named Sam and their daughter was named Ella. Their friends were shocked to hear about Sam&Ella in the Christmas letter.

Muffins spelled backwards is what you do when you take them out of the over.

Good moms let you lick the beaters. Great moms turn them off first.

Health

A priest, an imam, and a rabbit walk into a blood drive. The rabbit says, "I think I'm a type-O".

My friend keeps saying "Cheer up, it could be worse, you could be stuck underground in a hole full of water." I'm sure he means well.

I was looking for breath spray and accidentally got deodorant. Now I speak with a weird Axe scent.

What goes ha ha ha thump? A man laughing his head off.

Whenever I try to eat healthy a chocolate bar looks at me and snickers.

What do you call a group of rabbits walking away? A receding hare line.

Everyone was excited that 2020 was ending, but forgot that the year after 2021 is 2020 too.

You've gotta hand it to short people, because they can't reach it.

What's the inventor of hand sanitizer doing right now? He's rubbing his hands.

An old man fell into a well. Guess he just didn't see that well.

To whoever stole my glasses: I will find you. I have contacts.

Dr. Pepper didn't go to medical school. He's a fizzicist.

A knighted mummy with a cold is called Sir Cough A Gus.

A belt made of watches is a waist of time.

Before my surgery, the anesthesiologist offered to knock me out with gas or a boat paddle. It was an ether / oar situation.

The nurse came in and said "Doc, there's a man in the waiting room who thinks he's invisible. What should I tell him?" "Tell him I can't see him today."

Glass coffins – will they be popular? Remains to be seen.

I've started telling everyone about the health benefits of eating dried grapes. It's all about raisin awareness.

Turning vegan would be a big missed steak.

Life is short. If you can't laugh at yourself, call me and I will.

My mood ring is missing and I'm not sure how I feel about that.

Kleptomaniacs always take things literally.

Try resistance training. Refuse to go to the gym.

Looking back, I really hurt my neck.

Does the name Pavlov ring a bell?

Condoms should be used on every conceivable occasion.

What's the definition of a will? It's a dead giveaway.

The man who fell into an upholstery machine is fully recovered.

When Covid started, they said to wear a mask and gloves if you go out. I went grocery shopping and noticed that everyone else seemed to be wearing clothes.

"Incontinence hotline, please hold."

The nose is in the middle of the face because it's the scenter.

Life is sexually transmitted.

A cartoonist was found dead in his home. Details are sketchy.

England has no kidney bank, but it does have a Liverpool.

I didn't like my beard at first, but then it grew on me.

When you get a bladder infection, urine trouble.

I used to be indecisive. Now I'm not so sure.

The cemetery is such a great place that people are dying to get in there.

A small boy swallowed some coins and was taken to the hospital. When his grandmother telephoned to ask how he was, the nurse said "no change yet".

A Buddhist refused Novocain during a root canal. He wanted to transcend dental medication.

At age 4 success is not peeing in your pants.
At age 12 success is having friends.
At age 16 success is having a driver's license.
At age 20 success is having sex.
At age 35 success is having money.
At age 50 success is having money.
At age 60 success is having sex.
At age 70 success is having a driver's license.
At age 75 success is having friends.
At age 80 success is not peeing in your pants.

An adult is a person who has stopped growing at both ends and is now growing in the middle.

A beauty parlor is where women curl up and dye.

What's the difference between bird flu and swine flu? One requires tweetment and the other requires oinkment.

How many psychiatrists does it take to change a light bulb? One, but the bulb has to want to change.

When you replace I with We, Illness becomes Wellness.

The number of people older than you never goes up.

If humans have different blood types, do mosquitoes see us as different flavors?

If you have to wear both mask and glasses, you may be entitled to condensation.

When you said life would get back to normal after June...Julyed.

Pets

Yesterday I spotted an albino Dalmatian. It was the least I could do for the poor guy.

What kind of dog can jump higher than a building? Any dog. Buildings can't jump.

What did the snail say when he climbed on the tortoise's back? Wheeeeeee...

Dogs can't operate MRI scanners, but catscan.

Around Christmastime the post office becomes very discriminatory. They deliver hundreds of catalogs, but no dogalogs.

A chicken crossing the road is just poultry in motion.

I named my dogs Rolex and Timex. They're watch dogs.

It's very expensive to build a henhouse, because you have to use pullet-proof glass.

The Energizer Bunny was arrested and charged with battery.

A dog gave birth to puppies near the road and was cited for littering.

Two silkworms had a race and ended up in a tie.

Animal puns quack me up.

Well, this is hawkward!

I asked a librarian if she had any books about Pavlov's dogs or Schrodinger's cat. She said it rang a bell, but she wasn't sure if it was there or not.

A milking stool has only 3 legs, because the cow has the udder.

The dog who runs in front of a car gets tired. The one who runs behind gets exhausted.

Fish are easy to weigh because they have their own set of scales.

Quit hounding me about my bad puns. You're barking up the wrong tree.

Where does a dog go if its tail falls off? To the re-tail store.

A dog's favorite Pink Floyd album is "The Bark Side of the Moon".

How do you keep a dog from barking in the street? Put him in a barking lot.

We took our dog on a picnic, but he turned it into a bark-B-Q.

Anything is paw-sible when you have a dog.

My dog's not fat, he's just a little Husky.

The dog catcher sings while he picks up strays: "You Ain't Nothin' but a Pound Dawg".

It's raining cats and dogs. That's fine, as long as it doesn't reindeer.

Dachshunds always nap in the shade because they don't like being hot dogs.

People who hate dogs are re-pug-nant.

I want a pet duck, but I hear they come with a huge bill.

My pet crocodile needs help. Should I give him gatorade?

I have a pet tree. It's like a pet dog, but the bark is quieter.

I went into a pet shop and said, "I would like a pet for my wife." The owner said, "I'm sorry, we don't do swaps."

A porcupine with no quills would be pointless.

I don't go out much anymore. I tell people it's because I just bought a pet cow. I've been milking that excuse for weeks.

I fell asleep with my pet bunny in bed. I woke up with the hare standing up on the back of my neck.

Geography

We all know where the Big Apple is, but does anyone know where the Minneapolis?

If we all started driving pink cars, America would become a pink-car-nation.

No matter how kind you are, German kids are kinder.

My 4-year-old has been learning Spanish all year and still can't say the word for please, which I think is pretty poor for four.

Yesterday I purchased a world map, gave my wife a dart, and said "throw this and wherever it lands, I'm taking you for a vacation." So we're spending three weeks behind the refrigerator.

We should have known the USSR was collapsing. There were lots of red flags.

I'm not sure of the best thing about Switzerland, but the flag is a big plus.

Our mountains aren't just funny – they're hill areas.

If the world didn't suck, we'd all fall off.

Do people in Australia call the rest of the world "Up Over"?

Those who jump off a bridge in Paris are in Seine.

A local area network in Australia is a LAN down under.

Because of inflation, they had to rename some states. We now have Elevenessee, Califivenia, and Washingtwelve.

The ocean can't run all over the land because it's tide.

The Indians were here first because they had reservations.

I like Ohio because it offers all four seasons – sometimes all in one day.

I thought I saw an eye doctor on an Alaskan island, but it turned out to be an optical Aleutian.

Geology rocks, but geography is where it's at.

Which US state has the smallest soft drinks? Minisoda.

What did Tenna-see? She saw what Arkan-saw.

Where has Ora-gone? She's taking Okla-home.

How did Wiscon-sin? She stole a New-brass-key.

What did Della-wear? She wore a New Jersey.

What did Io-weigh? She weighed a Washing-ton.

Where did Ida-hoe? She hoed in Mary-land.

What did Missy-sip? She sipped her Mini-soda.

What did Connie-cut? She cut her shaggy Maine.

What did Ohi-owe? She owed her Texas.

How did Flora-die? She died of Missouri.

Hungary? Russian to the kitchen and Czech the fridge.

School

Double negatives are a no-no in English.

The teacher was expounding upon the idea that a double negative is actually a positive, but a double positive is never a negative. From the back of the room, a small voice said "yeah, yeah".

Did you hear about the kidnapping at school? It's okay, the teacher woke her up.

I have a wooden pencil that was owned by Shakespeare. He chewed it a lot, and I can't tell if it's a 2B or not 2B.

Writing my name in cursive is my signature move.

What do you say to comfort a friend who's struggling with grammar? There, their, they're.

Well, to be Frank, I'd have to change my name.

I'm friends with only 25 letters of the alphabet. I don't know Y.

Don't let anyone call you average. That's just mean.

A book hit my head and I've only my shelf to blame.

Terrible summer for Humpty Dumpty but he had a great fall.

He had a photographic memory that was never developed.

We're going on a class trip to the Coca-Cola factory. I hope there's no pop quiz.

The cross-eyed teacher lost her job because she couldn't control her pupils.

Broken pencils are pointless.

Light travels faster than sound, so some people appear bright until you hear them speak.

A rubber band pistol was confiscated from algebra class because it was a weapon of math disruption.

A backwards poet writes inverse.

The high school drama club put on a production that was all about puns. It was a play on words.

I'm reading a horror story in Braille. Something bad is going to happen…I can feel it.

Parallel lines have so much in common, it's a shame they'll never meet.

I don't trust stairs because they're always up to something.

Whoever invented knock-knock jokes should be given a no-bell prize.

We're living thru stuff that kids will cheat about on tests in 30 years.

Some classmates are such treasures you just want to bury them.

I hate peer pressure, and so should you.

If your friend has no boat dock, he's a friend without pier.

My friend David has his ID stolen. Now he's just Dav.

I'm going to start collecting highlighters, mark my words.

Beekeeping

Bee it ever so bumble, there's no place like comb.

When bees move to a new hive, they have a house-swarming party.

When a bee flies in high humidity it makes its hair all wild, so it becomes a frizz-bee.

What kind of bee can't make up its mind? A may-bee.

How does a bee straighten its disheveled hair? With a honey- comb.

I asked a beekeeper for a dozen bees. He gave me 13, saying "that's a freebee."

If you find someone with 10,000 bees marry them. You'll know they are a keeper.

I tried beekeeping, but I broke out in hives. Now I'm SKEPticle about the whole idea.

Wasps are just wannabees.

Church

A psychologist analyzed the biblical story of Moses, and concluded that when his mom set him adrift in a basket he was in de'Nile.

Skeletons can't play church music because they don't have organs.

Never buy flowers from a monk. Only you can prevent florist friars.

I was daydreaming in church about the bugs in my garden, when the priest, an avid gardener himself, shocked me back into the present by standing up and saying, "lettuce spray".

If you don't pay your exorcist, you'll get repossessed.

(Spoken with a Kentucky drawl...) The three wise men were first responders. It says right thar' in the Bible that they come from a'far.

Noah was the first electrician. He made the ark light on Mount Ararat.

The Supreme Court has ruled that there cannot be a Nativity scene on Capitol Hill this Christmas season. This isn't for a religious reason. They simply have not been able to find three wise men in Washington. The search for a virgin also continues. There was no problem, however, finding enough asses to fill the stable.

How does Moses make his tea? Hebrews it.

How do you make holy water? Boil the Hell out of it.

Going to church doesn't make you a Christian any more than standing in a garage makes you a car.

The secret of a good sermon is to have a good beginning and a good ending, and to have the two as close together as possible.

Atheism is a non-prophet organization.

When cannibals ate a missionary, they got a taste of religion.

Incense…holy smoke!

Mahatma Gandhi walked barefoot most of the time, developing calluses on his feet. He ate very little, which made him rather frail, and with his odd diet, he had bad breath. This made him a super callused fragile mystic hexed by halitosis.

When Noah built the Ark, he made the doors too low. When he loaded the animals he had the world's first giraffic jam.

Does anyone need an ark built? Because I Noah guy....

I directed the handbell choir at my church, but in my day job as an electrical engineer I learned that I really didn't want to be a good conductor.

Teenagers are God's revenge. God looked down and said, "Let's see how they feel about it when they create someone in their image who denies their existence."

The agnostic dyslexic insomniac lay awake nights wondering if there is a dog.

Transportation

Norway paints a barcode on the side of every one of their ships. When they return to port, they can Scandinavian.

I tried to sue the airline for misplacing my baggage. I lost my case.

Pirates can never finish the alphabet, because they always get lost at C.

They installed a speed bump on our street. I'm slowly getting over it.

If your car was 100% made of wood, it probably wooden work.

A bicycle can't stand on its own because it's two tired.

I've been in many places, but never in Cahoots. You can't go alone. You have to be in Cahoots with someone.

I've never been in Cognito. I hear no one recognizes you there.

I would like to go to Conclusions, but you have to jump, and I'm not too athletic anymore.

You don't know how fast you were going? That means I can write anything I want on the ticket.

At the bottom of the Bermuda Triangle is a wreck tangle.

The Eskimo got cold in his kayak, so he lit a fire. It sank, proving you can't have your kayak and heat it too.

I had a dream about mufflers, and woke up exhausted.

Politics

The problem with political jokes is they sometimes get elected.

Puns about communism aren't funny unless everyone gets them.

Limit politicians to two terms – one in office, and one in prison.

In democracy your vote counts. In feudalism your count votes.

I dropped out of Communism class because of lousy Marx.

We could certainly slow the aging process down if it had to work its way thru Congress.

Politicians are like bullies. They take all you'll allow them to take, then hurt you when you complain.

Politics is the gentle art of getting votes from the poor, and campaign funds from the rich, by promising to protect each from the other.

Politicians and diapers should be changed often, and for the same reason.

Aviation

An optimist invented the airplane. A pessimist invented the parachute.

The big fan on the front of the airplane is to cool the pilot. Just watch him sweat when it stops spinning!

Good judgement comes from experience, and experience comes from bad judgement.

I tried to catch some fog, but I mist.

The only time you have too much fuel is when you are on fire.

If the wings are traveling faster than the fuselage it has to be a helicopter, and therefore unsafe.

When one engine fails on a twin-engine aircraft, you always have enough power left to get you to the scene of the crash.

You know that your landing gear is up and locked when it takes full power to taxi to the terminal.

You don't need a parachute to skydive. You only need a parachute to skydive twice.

No matter how much you push the envelope it'll still be stationery.

The flying regulations forbid reckless operation. The FAA wants us all to fly wreckfully.

A vulture boards an airliner carrying two dead raccoons. The flight attendant says "I'm sorry sir, only one carrion per passenger".

My wife and I have agreed to not talk about my addiction to flying. It's a soar subject.

I love aviation jokes, but they always seem to go over people's heads.

I can't believe I'm almost finished with my pilot's license. The time has just flown by.

There's an abandoned building outside Cleveland labeled "Aviation High School". Looks like the idea didn't take off.

I had to take an eye exam and colorblindness test for my flight medical. I passed with flying colors.

A plane that flies backwards is a receding airline.

If you wear a watch on an airplane, time flies.

I selected airplane mode and threw my phone, but it didn't fly.

When the pilot began lying about his flying, he went into a tale spin.

A pilot who has never been lost will tell you other lies too.

Maintain social distancing – keep the planes at least 6′ apart.

www.ingramcontent.com/pod-product-compliance
Lightning Source LLC
Chambersburg PA
CBHW070426080426
42450CB00030B/1521